Words Written in the Dark

A story of love
& heartache…
but mostly love.
Self-love.

by Alexandria Rose Rizik

Words Written in the Dark

This is for you. *You* being anyone who needs these words, can connect with them, and appreciates their value.

Also, for my grandpa, Vaskan…you loved my poetry because you understood it and were a poet too. Thank you for passing this gift down to me.

Acknowledgements

This book is very special to me…for a lot of reasons. These poems (written over the course of four years) are tidbits of memories —beautiful ones and messy ones — frozen moments in time, they are the healing powers that got me through periods of anxiety, grief, heartache, etc. They are also proof that I am stronger than I realize, that I am capable of so much, and that all people alike *deserve* to be happy. So, without further ado, I'd like to thank a few individuals who pushed me during it all…

Thank you to my dad who is always so encouraging of my sisters and I and supporting our dreams.

For my mother, I want to thank you for always standing by my side during dark moments filled with so much anxiety and angst. You made my sisters and I the strong women we are.

I want to thank my sisters — my heaven-sent soulmates, who I couldn't function on a daily basis without.

Thank you to my life-coach, Howard Falco, who is such an inspiration to me and is constantly guiding me along this roller coaster ride called life!

Much thanks to Patrick Adams for always helping me to bring my literary visions to life — and making it seem so effortless in doing so.

I want to thank my family! And all those near and dear to my heart that support my passion for writing and who love me unconditionally. You've appreciated the

Words Written in the Dark

heart I wear on my sleeve & for that...I am forever grateful.

For my beautiful, sweet niece...thank you for changing my life and opening my eyes.

Thank you to Miles King for being there for me and always staying a true friend. You've helped me grow so much!

For the ultimate yoga guru, Matthew Ricci! Your yoga, meditation, & friendship helped me to manage anxiety during times when I couldn't even function.

Thank you, Hoang Loc, for your raw and stunning photography.

Lastly, thank you to the ones who've broken my heart and been my muse — without you, most of these poems wouldn't exist.

Copyright © 2019 by Alexandria Rizik
Published by Patrick Adams Books, LLC
All rights reserved. No part of this book may be reproduced without the written permission from the author.
ISBN-13: 978-0-9988416-8-7

Words written in the dark,
once upon a rainy evening…
nostalgia pouring upon us,
the fine moon looking down
giving us light,
but we neglect it
and continue to wonder
what went wrong.
It's so hard to see what we
wrote, when words are written
in the dark.

Words Written in the Dark

i. Reality

ALEXANDRIA RIZIK

"Reality"

Why is it that we tell people
we love them when we are drunk?
Is it our true feelings that we have been
holding back and wish to share?
Or is it another reality,
just like our dreams at night
in which our minds have an affair?

Kiss me sweet soul,
while I am awake,
while I am drunk,
and while I sleep
so that all three of my realities are in sync.

"Loss"

People say that love hurts,
but it isn't love that hurts —
it is the loss of love.

ALEXANDRIA RIZIK

"Gravity"

Nothing is for certain —
except the power of gravity and
the strength from love.

"Addiction"

Sometimes love can turn into an addiction,
only the drug and dealer are one in the same.

"Connection"

I surrendered to the connection
between me and you,
to the pleasurable pain that only
true lovers knew.

"Real"

You said you would always love me
and then you ran away.
When you came back, I thought
things would be different
but you were still afraid —

Of love, of happiness, and all the
other ways I make you feel.
You hide from the things that
you know are real…

"Rhythm"

I love you in every way a person
can love another;
as a first love, last love and an
everything in between love,
as a friend, a confidant, and a
person.
My heart beats to the rhythm of
your voice.

"Easier"

He thought the grass would be
greener on the other side;
but it wasn't,
there was just less to trim
which made it easier for him.

ALEXANDRIA RIZIK

"Laugh"

If you can't laugh at yourself
then you must be boring as shit.

"Moon"

I look up at the moon
and think of you
and then I wonder if you look up
and think of me too.

ALEXANDRIA RIZIK

"Space"

The scary thing about space is
wondering if distance will make
the heart grow fonder
or make the mind forget.

"Bitter"

And with every word
you fell like leaves from a tree,
leaving me bare and vulnerable before a bitter winter.

ALEXANDRIA RIZIK

"Living"

When you finally come to the
realization
that you are not here
to change the behavior of others,
or even comprehend it,
you will start living.

"Impressed"

And even when I caught your curveball,
you weren't impressed.

ALEXANDRIA RIZIK

"Alcohol"

Love is like alcohol;
the more you drunk you are,
the worse the hangover.

"Six"

God has his timing.
God has his reasons.
Be patient and pray on.
The world could have been created
in a single day,
He chose six.

"Galaxy"

Your soul burns like the blazing
sun,
keeping us warm when night is to
come.
Your heart glows like the moon,
shining upon us even when we lose ourselves
in the darkness.
Your mind sparkles like the stars,
intoxicating me with theories on
the depth of life.
You are a whole galaxy of things
to me.

"Lost"

If something is never lost,
how could it ever be found?
So remember,
it's okay to lose yourself
once in a while
for at the very least,
you will discover where you stand
in the crowd.

ALEXANDRIA RIZIK

"Enough"

We rarely saw eye to eye and
we didn't have much in common
except that we were madly
and foolishly
in love —
and that was enough.

"Time"

If love could tell time,
it would tell us to hurry.

"Tragedy"

Does she cross your mind when I'm with you?
Do you feel alright with me close to you?
Does she know that you were mine first?
Does she know this happens every time?
'Cause you'll always be mine.

Now everything you said
is stuck in my head,
not just a memory —
the whole story.
It's the story of us.
It's a story of lust.
What a tragedy.

"Calories"

Love comes and goes,
calories are forever.

"Eclipse"

The sun always seemed to fall asleep
as the moon awoke,
the timing never quite right.

But one night
for no good reason,
the sun and moon aligned.

A total solar eclipse lit up the darkness.
The tides were higher
and the winds were stronger
and the sky looked just a little lovelier.

And that showed the world
how magical the timing of life
could potentially be.

"Wander"

Sometimes our hearts belong in a city,
but we have to wander the world
to find our way back home.

ALEXANDRIA RIZIK

"Friday Nights, Wine, & the Moon"

How could it be,
that after everything that has happened,
that after the way we tortured each other's souls,
the mention of your name
still reminds me of everything lovely in life,
like Friday nights, wine, and the moon?

"Faith"

To have fear
is to have no faith.

ALEXANDRIA RIZIK

"Fire"

And when you find yourself in
the darkness of the woods
is when you learn to start your
own fires.

"Invest"

Would you keep investing in a
company
without any return?
Why should your relationships be
any different?

"Radio"

The timing of us
is like that tragic moment you
pull up
to your house
just as your favorite song
comes on the radio…

Do you keep on driving? Or just park and walk inside?

Words Written in the Dark

"Beating"

And when you feel paralyzed
from your heart's aching,
remember that it hasn't stopped
beating
and time will keep moving
forward,
with or without you,
so you might as well move with
it.

"Delusional"

I thought you were delusional
until I realized no one can
actually be "delusional" — we just
have ulterior perceptions
creating a variety of realities.
If everyone's reality was the
same,
we'd all get up at the same time,
put on the same pair of clothes,
have the same job,
and love the same person.
And I'm not okay with anyone else
loving you.

Words Written in the Dark

"Rules"

The premise
of our existence
should not revolve around
the rules society has made for us.

If no one every challenged the norm,
we'd still be running around in
loin cloths,
hunting for our lunch.

Make your own rules.

ALEXANDRIA RIZIK

"Settle"

Fear dances around in the hearts
of the weak,
so they settle for settling.

"Endure"

He was the disease,
he was the cure.
He was the pain that I wanted to
endure.

He was the question,
he was the answer.
He was my never happy after.

He was the shark,
he was the bait.
He was supposed to be my fate.

"Madness"

We rode our bikes down the rocky path.
You stopped when it got dark
as I kept pushing forward
through all of the madness.
When I turned around,
you had retreated back to your safe place
where it did not rain,
but nor did the sun ever shine.

"Pen"

If your favorite pen runs out of ink,
don't force it into working.
It's time to write a new poem
with a new pen.

"Cheesy"

You're a cheesy metaphor
with a glass of wine,
you're a hundred memories
that are all mine.
You stimulate the heart
just like caffeine,
you bring out the best and worst
in me.

"Tug-of-War"

I'm sorry it ended this way,
this game of tug-of-war where no one
wanted to give.
Now there's no rope,
no game,
no fun.
I miss it when we were young.

ALEXANDRIA RIZIK

"Wild"

My heart was wild and reckless,
yours calm and tamed.
Somehow they met in the middle
and when it all came crumbling
down in front of us,
as it always goes,
only the wild child could be
blamed.

"Class"

For one to become a classic,
they must have class.

"Doors"

You slammed the door on me,
leaving me to open new doors
that led to better opportunities.
Now you want to see what it looks
like inside,
leaving you searching for
something you threw aside.

"Words"

Small souls
use big words
to appear superior.

Strong souls
use any word
that they think might touch
the heart of another.

ALEXANDRIA RIZIK

"Hope"

I slept in the mud
of the rainy night
waiting for you
to never return
just as promised.
I lied when I asked you to leave,
desperately and secretly
hoping you'd come searching
and find me
as the sun peaked through
the gray clouds,
giving us a sprinkle of hope.

"Deeper"

Let's jump into the ocean
together
and dive down
into something deeper,
something deeper than our
lungs can bear.
And if we never see the surface
again,
at least we can say
we felt something
so deep
that it took our breath
away.

"Dreamland"

I fall asleep to his eyes,
only to fall into dreamland
where I can find yours.
For hours you take me on
magic carpet rides
through a town I've never known
until I must awake again
to those eyes I have yet to want
but don't.
I love him,
I really do,
but I will never love anyone
like I love you.

"Late"

I want to talk again
but you're too caught up
in all the reasons we fell apart;
the things we said
and the things
we did not.
The days we spent silent
and the days
we spent in deep thought
over if this was worth it
or if we should just
throw it all away
before it turned into
a mess.
I guess we are too late.

ALEXANDRIA RIZIK

"Rosé"

A glass of rosé a day
keeps the bull shit away.

"Lost in love"

Get lost in love,
forget the map.

ALEXANDRIA RIZIK

"Greatness"

Everyone has greatness
within them.
Don't waste your time
with anyone who doesn't see
yours.

"Reincarnates"

Our love story
reincarnates when
I'm drunk.

ALEXANDRIA RIZIK

"Bullet & Arrow"

Cupid's arrow
and your bullet
hit my heart
all at once,
leaving me
painfully in love.

"Existed"

I think
the hardest pill to swallow
is accepting that
the love story between
you and another being,
may not just be over,
but quite possibly never
existed…
because the person you loved
never did.

"Black & White"

Red wine.
Black and white films.
On my big grey couch.
Just me and you.
My heart palpitates
as your hand moves closer to mine,
the wine has kicked in —
what a dangerous interaction
of substances,
love and wine.
My heart doesn't know whether it should
speed up
or slow down.
This buzz has got me feeling
all sorts of colors.

"Tea"

Birds chirp
outside my window
as the sun shines through.
A cup of tea
in hand,
each sip
caresses my soul
with a different memory
of you.

ALEXANDRIA RIZIK

"Photosynthesis"

We were two flowers
in a garden,
resting under the sun.
But we were in two
different phases;
I,
already grown into myself
and ready to pollinate
and
you,
you were still undergoing
photosynthesis,
trying to root yourself
into this world.

"Sand"

You were the ocean
and I, the sandy shore.
You ran your waves
through every grain of my being
only to retreat back
to where you started.
Like the sand patiently waits,
I remain still, as you
constantly
return back to me —
prepared for you to leave again.
But I always know,
it isn't for long.

ALEXANDRIA RIZIK

"Self-love"

Sometimes
letting go
is love.
Self-love.

"Somewhere"

It's like you were
always there
even when you weren't
even before I met you
even after you left
you were there
somewhere
in my heart or soul
or in my bones
you were there.

"Alive"

They say
anything that is
alive
will eventually
die,
it is the nature of
life.
But I think
our love
will prove
all of these troubled earthlings
wrong.

"Magic"

It seems
apropos
to say magic exists
only in the hearts
of those who
believe in it,
the same way
love does.
Maybe
in a sense,
love is magic
and the problem is
not enough of us
believe.

ALEXANDRIA RIZIK

"Disguised"

Most blessings
are initially disguised
as a loss.
Don't worry,
your tears will
flood over into
an ocean of success.
Soon.

"Chemistry"

You were my oxygen,
I,
your lithium;
together we burned a red flame
only we would ever know.
It was that kind of beautiful
chemistry.

ALEXANDRIA RIZIK

"Kiss & Bite"

Kiss my heart
and bite my lip,
not the other way around.

"Buzz"

The worst part
about our sudden
goodbye,
is having to finish this
bottle of wine
all by myself.

It's a different kind of buzz.

ALEXANDRIA RIZIK

"Ego"

Every night
I deceive my precious
ego
and pray
that this isn't
the end.

"Sky Kisses"

Kiss me passionately
the way the sky kisses
the mountains, no matter if
the sun is shining
or darkness is arriving.

ALEXANDRIA RIZIK

"Depth"

Use your experiences to create depth,
in your heart to love more,
in your mind to learn more,
in your gaze to observe more,
and in your soul to feel more.
Create depth
and you will attract the lovers
of the world
and repel the haters.
Create depth.

"Wind"

Sometimes
a wind will cast your scent
through the air
and a million little memories
drift to the front of my mind.

ALEXANDRIA RIZIK

"Orbiting"

I was earth,
you my sun,
my light;
everything I did
revolved around you
but even so,
you left parts of me
dark.
But it was the parts
that you lit up
that kept me orbiting
around you
because
I craved your heat.

"Guaranteed"

Nothing is guaranteed in life,
except the things we give
ourselves;
like self-love
and happiness.

"Underdog"

Love,

your cruel punishment
to me.
Like a shower
that goes from steaming hot
to ice cold.
But I crave it
and its pleasurable pain.
Its shock.
A flower
that smells like a wild animal.
But I like the unusualness of it.
Someone has to love the underdog —
someone has to teach him how to feel.

"Love & Heartbreak"

Love
and
heartbreak
are like twins,
one an angel
and the other, evil.
But you can't have one without the other,
and although they don't get along,
they are still blood.

Let us be the ones to distance them for good.

ALEXANDRIA RIZIK

"The Coffee Shop"

Wooden tables
surrounded by empty
and full
chairs.
Computers and headphones
and empty stares.
Music that bellows
without any dancing,
people chatting
and couples romancing.
A sip of coffee,
a pour of tea,
does anyone realize
that we are spinning around on a rock
at 25 degrees?

"Melting"

And one day,
I see myself melting
into your arms,
the same way
the sun melts into the ocean
every night
before she falls asleep.

ALEXANDRIA RIZIK

"Mad"

Darling,
let's be mad for each other.

I can feel your heart beating
in my bones.

"Thinking"

Thinking is not a bad thing,
no,
not a bad thing at all.
But don't let your thoughts paddle
too far out into the ocean
for your mind might get lost
at sea.

"Words"

Imagine a world without words,
how would you express to your loved ones
that you love them?
Maybe that's what we need;
a day where no words existed.
Only actions.
Only love.

"Reasons"

I think about if we never existed
and how you could have never
broken my heart
and all of the poems
that would have never been written...
Maybe everything does happen for a reason.

"Chances"

Chances are,
if you're still thinking about them,
they're still thinking about you too.

"Last First Time"

We lay in the grass,
gazing above,
our fingers intertwined
as our clammy palms touch for
the last first time;
pink clouds
shaped like unicorns
painted against
a powder blue sky
above the black mountains.
I like our mystical world.

ALEXANDRIA RIZIK

"Red Sea"

I'm no longer sad
reminiscing on the idea
that you and I are over.
We may not forever be in each other's arms
but we will forever live on in my heart
and what a beautiful place
that is to reside,
for you will always have a view of
an enchanting, red flowing sea.

"The Call"
(For my papa)

I think back to my
last conversation with you,
to the last time I laid eyes on you.
You were sick,
your breath barely there.
How I wish I hugged you tighter,
how I wish I took a little longer
to say goodbye,
for I surely wasn't aware
that I would be so blind-sided
on a Tuesday.
I'd seen you just a few hours
before,
before we got the call.
Now a part of me will always be
missing,
but you can have it
because you gave me,
and all of this family,
so much more.

"Pretend"

Can we play pretend
and build a fort in my bedroom
and live in it together —
maybe not forever,
but just until midnight?
And we can pretend
that the moonlight shining in
is a moon living in the Parisian skies.
And maybe,
just maybe,
after all this pretending,
we'll open our eyes
and be there,
hand in hand,
looking up at the stars,
talking about when we used to play pretend.

"Past Tense"

I see you in the pepperoni of my pizza,
I see you in the moon of the night,
I seek you at the bottom of the bottle,
I speak to you as I write.

These tidbits of memories
intoxicate me with everything we used to be
as I pen about us in the past tense —
the past is somewhere I never thought you would be.

ALEXANDRIA RIZIK

"Old Songs & First Loves"

Change is hard,
that's why we cling to
old songs
and first loves.

"Empty"

Empty wine bottles
memories filled to the rim
sit on the top shelf.

ALEXANDRIA RIZIK

"Tattoo"

I tattooed you
onto my heart
while I was still too young
to understand the repercussions.
But I don't regret you
like our parents told us,
no.
You were a part of my life
and I will forever
wear that tattoo
for the world to see.
You will always be a part of me.

"Cup of Galaxy"

You poured me a cup of your galaxy
and intoxicated me with stars.
They lit up my soul
with a love that made me feel spacey
as if my heart and mind collided like two stars
and my conscious being, now
a supernova.
Be my moon
and let's light up the night sky together.

ALEXANDRIA RIZIK

"October Sunday"

The window is open,
a slight breeze brushes through.
We're a little bit hungover
from that bottle of wine
the night before that we consumed.

We're not together
but I can feel your heart
beating somewhere inside of mine.
I smile as I sip on coffee,
memories flooding my mind

Just like a hurricane.
But I don't want this storm to end.
It is as if you are the rain
and the rainbow.

You make my heart scream with excitement,
pound with thunder,
and light up with lightning
but my mind —
my mind is calm
just like an overcast sky
on this beautiful October Sunday.

"The Moon"

Before you,
I saw the moon.

With you,
I was the moon.

After you,
I craved the moon.

ALEXANDRIA RIZIK

"Decaf"

Every sip of coffee
stimulates me
with the memories of our past.
Maybe I should try decaf.

"Poem"

I was going to write you a letter,
I was going to write you a song,
but both seemed too long.
I figured a sweet and simple poem
shall do,
that way I can sort through
all the small talk;
I just wanted you to know that
I love you.

ALEXANDRIA RIZIK

"Without You"

Enough time passed
to make me wonder
what I ever saw in you,
just like everyone said;
until I saw you again.
then I wondered
how so much time
had passed without you.

Words Written in the Dark

"Meaningless"

You heard meaningless words
as I spoke deep metaphors to you.

ALEXANDRIA RIZIK

"Vandalize"

We climbed up a lovely mountain,
only to vandalize it
with our heartache
and anger.

"Big Love"

She was a strong woman
with a big heart
and he was a weak man
with small hands.
He couldn't carry her love.

ALEXANDRIA RIZIK

"Dancing Shadows"

Our shadows held hands
even after our hearts danced
to different songs.

"You"

He pours me a glass,
the first sip tasting
a lot like you.
He pours me the rest of the bottle,
and he starts looking like you.

ALEXANDRIA RIZIK

"Stitched"

I stitched up
the hole in my heart —
the piece that you took with you —
with small piece of his.
Now he has a hole
and all I have is a bandage.
What is this cycle
that we call love?

"Orange Blossom"

You are an orange blossom
in a beautiful valley;
you smell as lovely
as you look
but I seem to be allergic
to you,
tearing up
with every breath of you
that I take in.

"Miles & Oceans & Mountains"

What's worse than
you leaving
and being miles
and oceans
and mountains apart,
is you leaving
and being down the street
only a block away
as if we are
miles
and oceans
and mountains apart.

"Arsonist"

It hasn't been that long
since I've seen your face,
but it feels like forever
because you left without a trace
of where you're going
or if you'll return.
You lit my heart on fire
like an arsonist
and let it burn.

ALEXANDRIA RIZIK

"Shooting Stars"

Can we lay in your room
and close our eyes
and pretend
that shooting stars are passing by?
I'd wish for us to stay like this
forever.

"Bug Bites"

Bug bites
from the night before.
Both of us covered
from head to toe.
There was something romantic
about sharing the same scars.
When we awoke,
it was a reminder of what had happened
only a few drunken hours before —
in the grass,
just you and I,
wine and secrets spilled
staining our hearts
as we were eaten alive…
just as our lips met
for the last first time.

ALEXANDRIA RIZIK

"Taste Buds"

Through time
we lose so much;
friends,
family,
pets,
old habits,
even our taste buds change;
but my feelings for you —
those forever remain the same.

"Hit & run"

We collided head on
but it wasn't an accident;
it was a hit and run.

ALEXANDRIA RIZIK

"How it was"

There comes a point
where so much has been
said and done
that there is no
going back;
it'll never be like
"how it was".

"Midnight in Paris"

Midnight in Paris,
in the back of your
car;
forget the
attractions,
I want to see your
heart.

ALEXANDRIA RIZIK

"Collided"

The stars didn't align for us—
they collided into one.

"Page 90"

His book laid
on his desk,
the corner of page
90
folded over
while his body now
rested underground
as if he was supposed to
have already finished
the book.

ALEXANDRIA RIZIK

"Inhale, Exhale"

I inhaled your soul
as you exhaled mine;
what is this issue
we have with time?

"Bottle Full of Bad Choices"

The burning feeling
down my throat,
into my chest —
a bottle full of
bad choices.

ALEXANDRIA RIZIK

"Roses, Violets, & Other Stupid Colors"

Roses are red,
violets are blue
but who gives a shit about colors,
if I can't be with you.

Words Written in the Dark

"Love Yourself"

In order to love this world,
we must love what the world
has given us...
in other words,
we must love
ourselves.

ALEXANDRIA RIZIK

"Unknown"

Love is a bright light
shining in your eyes,
blinding you
as you drive down the
road called "unknown".

"Raining Tears"

It poured and poured
& we swore and swore
until the sky no longer rained
and tears no longer fell.

ALEXANDRIA RIZIK

"With Closed Eyes"

And if we never shut
our eyes
and saw darkness,
kissing and dreaming
and loving
would never shine
so brightly…

"Broken Bones"

We danced until the moon
fell asleep
& the sun awoke.
We loved until our bones
ached
& our hearts broke…

"You Can't Run From Love"

When the right person comes along,
there will not be any chasing
for either parties
because no one
will be running
from the situation…

Words Written in the Dark

"Strange Lovers"

Strangers.
Friends.
Lovers.
Strangers…
It was that kind of dark poetry.

"Signs, love, & magic"

If you're looking for
a sign, look to the street.
If you're looking for
love, look in the mirror.
But darling,
if you are looking for magic,
stop looking
and start feeling.

"To Fall"

You want me
but you never call;
you're in love with me
but you're too afraid to
fall.

ALEXANDRIA RIZIK

"Memory-covered Coat"

I wish your scent
still covered this coat,
so that I could be covered in
memories of you.

"Goldfish"

Crunchy goldfish
as we tried to sober ourselves,
once upon a
romantically drunken
moonlit night…

ALEXANDRIA RIZIK

"Fallen Stars"

We fell apart
in the most beautiful of ways —
like the way the stars
fall from the sky,
leaving us with wishes…

"Messy side"

We all have a messy side,
a side we can't control.
We all have darkness
glowing in our soul.
We all have depth,
only one person will ever reach.
We all have lessons we have learned
that only mistakes can teach.

ALEXANDRIA RIZIK

"Your Planet"

It is your planet
that I desire
to reside on;
even if the sun never shines
and it rains for years to come.
It is the oxygen of
your world
that I crave to take a hit of.

"Organized Chaos"

We were chaos,
organized so well
that ever time
we fell apart
it looked like abstract art.

ALEXANDRIA RIZIK

"Used to"

I know you
may not be able to
give me all of the things
I am used to,
but I only want to become
used to
what the beat of your heart
sounds like
while lying in your arms.

I know you
may never be able to
buy me a castle,
but I only want to build
a fortress
together,
on a secluded island
that lies on a map
only we know of.

I know you
will probably not
be able to promise me forever
but today already seems long
enough
and I
will take any sliver
of a second
of this beautiful life

Words Written in the Dark

with you
that I may have.

I know you may
may not be able to
give me all of the things
I am used to,
but all I really want
is you.

ALEXANDRIA RIZIK

"Forgotten Melody"

It's twisted
how a
certain song
can take you back
to a whole other
time and place
that you forgot even
existed.

"The Clean Ending"

Endings are not always
a hurricane
or a tornado…
sometimes they are
a light sprinkle of rain,
cleansing the soul
from yesterday's
troubles.

ALEXANDRIA RIZIK

"OD on you"

I overdosed on heartbreak
and you watched the whole time…
you knew that I was addicted
to you,
as you kept injecting me with your beautiful lies.

Your false promises were my favorite high.

"Stripped"

I stripped down
to my soul,
and you,
to your heart —
love has a funny way
of making humans
get naked...
until all you can see
are blood and tears.

"It was love"

We had
our own version
of love —
it might not have been
what we wanted
or expected,
but surely enough,
it was love.

"Detour"

I'm not sure how long
our paths are meant to cross,
but I like this detour.

ALEXANDRIA RIZIK

"Grown"

I wish things were different
but they aren't —
I wish we were the same,
but we've grown apart.

"Too Far Gone"

Bruised and battered,
the boy who was born already shattered.
He drank and he smoked,
until he was numb and broke.
A sad existence indeed
but he didn't want to be freed.
Even when a girl came along
and sang him her heart's favorite song —
"I love you"
"I love you"
She sang it again,
but he was already too far gone
to be anything but friends…

ALEXANDRIA RIZIK

"You"

If you were a nobody
to everybody
I would still choose
you.

"Prayers & Poetry"

Dear God,
Thank you for the sign
and for taking away
what wasn't meant to be mine.

Thank you for the hope
and thank you for the ability to move on.
Thank you for helping me cope
and thank you for the people
who have come and gone.

ALEXANDRIA RIZIK

"Fall Apart"

I really do love you
with all of my heart —
even if time changes us
and we fall apart.

"Citrus Tree"

He kissed me underneath the citrus tree
one day, late at night.
But our minds were somewhere else,
maybe inside the pack of Miller Lite.
Friends for so long,
suddenly something else.
How could it be that feelings were there?
and we hadn't even known it until they were felt?

Now I sit in the spot
where it started,
only the sun is shining,
birds are chirping,
and we're not talking...

"The Easy Life"

You once had dreams like me
but you gave up and settled for the
easy life;
the job you dread,
and the wife you didn't plan to wed
but you did because it all
made sense.
Now life has got you beat
and you let it take its defeat,
and yeah, you're happy.
Or maybe you're just fine.
But sometimes you sit there
and wonder
in the midst of all the chaos,
what your life would be like
if I was yours and
you were mine.

ii. Reality Check

ALEXANDRIA RIZIK

"You and Me"

Love isn't Paris and fancy cars…
love is simply you & me,
you & me,
you & me,
wherever that may be.

Words Written in the Dark

"Lost it"

I've lost my mind
now and again,
but I always seem to find it
with you in the end.

"Not Like This"

Your pictures
aren't mine to "like",
even though you held me
in your arms so tight.

Our memories
aren't mine to tell,
because there is no more "us",
even though we made them so well.

This story
wasn't supposed to end,
at least not like this,
but maybe our paths will
meet again.

"Call me Crazy"

They call me crazy,
they say I have it all wrong.
They say I fall in love too easily
and that love doesn't last that long…

They say I fantasize too much,
and to get with reality.
But I have big dreams,
dreams that they are too afraid to see.

I can't help but see a unicorn
when they only see a mule.
They say perception is reality,
then you create your own and they change the rules.

ALEXANDRIA RIZIK

"Mary Jane"

I can't make you love me,
I can't make you care,
I can't force you to
put down the joint…
I wouldn't dare.

You're too addicted
to the chaos,
but never to me.

You'd rather feel
attached to Mary Jane
and her friends
because they set you free.

"For Love"

I've made a fool of myself for love
over and over again.
But I wouldn't change it for the sake of
how it all would end.

ALEXANDRIA RIZIK

"Come back to you"

If it's true,
it will come back to you…
but if it is not,
you will always keep the lessons
it taught.

"Summer's End"

Summer has ended
and so have we...
our love fell to the ground
just like these changing leaves.

But by springtime
our souls will be anew,
and leaves will have grown,
because people change just like seasons do.

ALEXANDRIA RIZIK

"It's Okay to Not be Okay"

It's okay
to not be okay...
But when tomorrow comes
remember it is a new day.

"Bent"

And just when
you think
you might break,
you'll bend so far back
that you'll rebound
back into shape.

"High, how are you?"

Out of all the drugs
that there are to get
high on...
your words are my favorite.

"Before I Knew Your Name"

I was
delicate & pure;
you were
wild and untamed.
I told you when I loved you,
while you just played games.

I was never bad enough for
you —
so I tried to change.
Fuck that. I'm removing these tattoos.
I like the "me" before I knew
your name.

ALEXANDRIA RIZIK

"Thinking of You"

Staring into space...
They ask me what's on my mind.
I tell them "nothing, I'm ok. I'm fine."

If they only knew...
I was thinking of you.

"Close to me"

You weren't the man
I made you out to be,
but you tried whenever
you were close to me...

ALEXANDRIA RIZIK

"Fixer"

I've been told I'm a fixer,
but is it true?
The one thing I wanted to fix but couldn't
so happened to be you...

"Broken Clock"

The broken clock,
ticks and tocks...
although it may be broken,
time doesn't stop.

ALEXANDRIA RIZIK

"Raindrops in my Coffee"

Raindrops in my coffee
as I walk to the car...
it tastes like nostalgia
although the memories seem so far.

Raindrops kissing the window,
the windshield wiping them away...
and although I crave your company,
I wish I could do the same.

"Warn Her"

And the scariest part is,
I don't know you
and never did
and neither does she
and she never will.

You give just enough of yourself
to make the other person give everything
and then you take it all with you...

I wish I could warn her...

ALEXANDRIA RIZIK

"Text Message Thread"

Your words satisfied me
like my favorite cup of tea,
they replayed through my head
like a book I wish I'd never read.

They seduced my heart
and turned my sadness into art.
Your words...they shouldn't have been said
but they were, and now I can't seem to erase the text
message thread.

"Night Birds"

Have you ever heard
the birds that chirp
in the midst of the night?
There is something about those birds,
something that makes it sweeter
to fall asleep.
They chirp among the moon,
among the stars,
among the darkness;
oh, what a gift
to sing so beautifully
even in the absence of light
when no one may be listening.

"Friend or Foe"

Rainy nights
at the drive-in theater...
Me and you.
The fogged-up windows
a symbol that our love is true.
Flashes of the film
in the background,
the sound on low,
now it is all just a memory
and I'm not sure
if you're a friend or foe.

"Dope AF"

Most of life's complexities
stem from the mind...
How do I look?
Am I enough?
Why don't they like me?

How about less questions
& more declarations!
I know I look dope af.
I'm more than enough for anyone
and everyone.
They don't like me
& that's their problem that
they have to deal with internally...

"Met Like This"

Could it be
that I might love you?
Even though our fingers
have never interlaced,
and our bodies have never known each other's
type of embrace?
Could it be
that I've fallen with a simple
"Hello"?
Or that I've been here all along
and now you're just noticing me even though we know
that this isn't the first time we met,
*but it may be the first time
we've met like this...*

"Not You"

They think I'm talking about you
but I'm talking about him now.

ALEXANDRIA RIZIK

"Fantasies"

I wonder if we'll ever
kiss
or if this is just
a fantasy full of hopes and temporary
bliss.

Words Written in the Dark

"Kiss me if I'm Right, Seduce me if I'm Wrong"

As I lie here
late at night,
thinking of you,
I have a feeling
even though we barely know each other
that you're thinking of me too...

*Kiss me if I'm right,
seduce me if I'm wrong...*

ALEXANDRIA RIZIK

"Hummingbird"

You inspire me
without even saying a word...
the way you flew into my heart so effortlessly
as if it was a flower
and you, a hummingbird.

"Liquid Courage"

I'm up,
thinking of you
& you're out somewhere,
thinking of me too.
I'm hyped on caffeine
& you're buzzed off Hennessy...
just enough liquid courage for you
to message me.

ALEXANDRIA RIZIK

"Craving"

They say
it takes 10 minutes
for a craving to pass;
but I don't think this longing for you
will ever go away...

"Tell Me What's Real"

I don't want bull shit
I want what's real,
don't tell me what I want to hear.
Tell me how you actually feel.

ALEXANDRIA RIZIK

"Howl"

When the wolf spoke...
she spoke only of the
night & what it felt like
to howl in the silence
of the darkness,
when everyone around her
chose to keep their voices down.

"Rebuilt"

I had to rebuild these halls,
after you set fire to these castle walls.

I had to start from scratch,
not sure if I'd ever get what I *was* back...

Now the kingdom is a little smaller,
and these walls are quite taller.

But now it is made of steel...not straws.

ALEXANDRIA RIZIK

"That is All I'll Say"

I'm trying to find the
right words,
to tell you how I feel.
I'm not sure if they'll be big or small,
but I can say, they will be real.

No, I don't love you —
but I might one day.
You gave me a sense of hope...
that is what I'll say.

You made me realize that I can feel again,
that everything I thought he was,
could be found in you, but even more so—
like a fairytale that doesn't have to end.

Thank you.

That is all I'll say.

"Love & Loyalty"

I don't need the big shiny diamond,
I just want your love & loyalty.
Why put a label on something
just to satisfy our society?

"Chase Me"

I want you to chase me,
like no other boy has ever done.
I want you to chase me
& make me run.

Chase me over the hills
and around the bend,
but make sure to catch up
so I can call you mine in the end...

"The Way You Do"

My biggest fear was
to end up without you...
now, my biggest nightmare
is to end up with anyone that acts the way you do.

ALEXANDRIA RIZIK

"Miracle"

Every moment is a miracle.
Don't forget that.

"Blue-less Skies"

If tomorrow our sky
is no longer blue...
then shit,
I hope I get to spend every blue-less day
with you.

ALEXANDRIA RIZIK

"An Empty Love"

Every night
we lie awake,
afraid that morning will come
and drugs will take your fate.

Your soul is all consumed
by a love that can never love you back,
yet we are the enemies...
I suppose that is part of having a disease that mentally
attacks.

I hope you find the strength
to reclaim your strength & climb out of this black hole.
At this point it'd be a miracle
to see you scrub these drugs from your soul.

But God sends us miracles every day...

"Entering & Leaving Love"

Falling,
walking,
running,
maybe it's a full sprint...
however you get there,
even if in a clumsy, drunken stupor,
when it is time to walk away,
do it with grace & integrity.

That is how you must enter and leave love.

ALEXANDRIA RIZIK

"Blooming"

And ironically,
the storm gave us
hope...
that maybe the lilacs
will bloom tomorrow.

Words Written in the Dark

"Opinion"

Love is an opinion...

ALEXANDRIA RIZIK

"Kiss me slowly, leave me quickly"

Kiss me slowly
so I remember it
even tomorrow,
but leave me quickly
so I may forget these lustful sorrows.

"Our Love is Art"

Let's be like that sculpture
you read about in books
and hear about from your mom's friend.
The one that is known
for generations to come...

You know that one
that left its legacy
somewhere in Italy;
a man and woman,
their bodies entangled,
and although they're hundreds
or maybe even thousands of years old...
their love looks frozen in time.

Let's be that sculpture
because our love is art...

"Not That Girl"

I struggle with the concept of forever
& what a commitment looks like
for you vs. for me...
I'm not one of those girls whose been planning her wedding
since she was five; I'm not that girl you see in the movie.

Although I write all of these rhymes
romanticizing this idea of "love" and "happily ever after",
I don't know if I could ever be dedicated to a lifetime
with anyone.
Maybe that's why might heart has been so broken; not
because of him.
But because of me.

"Bad Boys"

And then you get older
and the bad boys become
the boring boys;
Predictable in every move they make...
from the lies they tell, to the places they hang out.
Suddenly,
you're over it.

ALEXANDRIA RIZIK

"Without me, You're not Okay"

I just want to be someone's favorite person,
that's what I want to be.
I want someone who can be just walking down the road
and thinks of me.

I want to be needed
and I have a need to be wanted.
Is it so much to ask,
that without me, your heart may be haunted?

Just tell me you love my name...
Just tell me I'm your favorite dame.
I'll give you my all,
just promise without me, you're not okay.

"State of Grace"

And every time
you walk away,
you leave me
in a new state of grace...

ALEXANDRIA RIZIK

"Fire & Ice"

If you befriend a devil
in hopes of helping them find
their angel wings...
You'll soon realize
fire always burns ice
and in an attempt to convince you
of their purity,
they're actually giving you horns.

Words Written in the Dark

"Once upon a time…"

Once upon a time
a boy and girl fell in love,
they thought they'd found the one.
Then something went wrong…
they listened to all the people around them,
people who envied their love.
They broke up.
And nobody lived happily ever after.
In fact…
Nobody lived at all.

"Story of Us"

One day,
hundreds of years after
my stories have been written,
I hope kids in schools
are studying romantic tragedies
that came from my heart.
I hope they talk about my characters and cry,
the same way they discuss Shakespearean tragedies...

I hope they read the story of us...

"Clean"

Now I've got a clear mind,
no drinking or crazy nights.
So many things
that I forget,
blacked out on tequila & regret.

Now I'm clean
and you're not buzzing in my head,
like a little bee...
I'm over the sting.

I'm clean.
No more withdrawals of you.
No longer drunk on love,
just a little caffeine to get me through.

"Love you, love me"

I want to be with you on rainy days
when the skies are gloomy
and the pavement is wet.
I want to lie with you on the beach,
our bodies entangled on the sand.
I want to spend every holiday with you
and explain to distant relatives
how we met.
I want to have deep conversations
about faraway galaxies that haven't
been discovered yet.

*I want to love you
and to know that you love me too…*

"Muddy Feet"

You traced your muddy feet
all over me,
leaving dirt covering my body
long after you left.
And even though I'm clean now,
whenever people look my way
I'm scared of what they'll see...
Yes, this is what you've done to me.

Done to me mentally.

ALEXANDRIA RIZIK

"Internal Storm"

Some days
I lose the fight—
The fight to be happy.
Some may know what I mean,
some may not.
Those with the prettiest masks
are the ones who've fought.
We hide behind happy faces,
but inside is like a storm
...a storm of insecurity and paranoia,
Over analytical thoughts, like your heart is torn.

Like a terrorist attack inside my mind,
these thoughts they come crashing through...
Self-deprecating,
they make sure to get you.
Misunderstood—
or maybe that's just the thoughts again.
I'll never know.
But today is a good day,
who knows about tomorrow.

When did I become like this?
It seems like a blur...
Somewhere between childhood and adulthood,
we learn that life can hurt...

I wish I wasn't like this,
believe me.

Words Written in the Dark

I know my emotions can be a lot to handle.
And all I want is to be happy.

That is all...

*And since I don't speak well,
I thought I'd write about it.*

ALEXANDRIA RIZIK

"First real love"

In this lifetime
you will fall
for your first love...
but then you will fall out of it.

Eventually...
Times goes by
and you'll stumble upon your
first real love.

One is here to teach,
the other to stay.

"Experiences"

I don't have all of the answers,
I only have experiences.
Those of which
I can only hope
that you may relate…

I've gone through
all sorts of
phases;
All of which have
led me
here…

People say
they're glad I went through it,
but
sometimes,
I wish I could've learned
by listening
instead of talking.

ALEXANDRIA RIZIK

"Then & Now"

Love isn't the same to me now
as it was then…
when I was just a young girl,
playing pretend.

Love is no longer about another…
love is who I am and what I encompass
within myself.
Love is not he or we,
it is me.

If I can't love myself,
how can I love anyone else?
How can I properly be?

Love is more than a vow,
a song,
a feeling,
or a ceremony…

Love is how you treat yourself.

"126 Days"

126 days since our last goodbye.
Funny how time seems to keep moving,
even when it sees me cry.

3024 hours since I last heard you say my name,
What if I never hear you say it again?
Not even in vein?

I'm sure another 181440 minutes will pass away
and I'll mourn the moments we collected & let decay.

But I know it will all be okay?
At least that's what I keep telling myself...
Minute by minute.
Hour by hour.

Day by Day.

ALEXANDRIA RIZIK

"Exotic"

Mary Jane
Nora
Crystal—
You left me for these girls
With such exotic names...

They intoxicate you
with a buzz I can't give.
But what happened to love?
Is that no longer enough?

Nothing is enough for an addict.
Not even the high that
Mary Jane
Nora
And crystal provide.

I wish you'd find a way to stay clean
& clear your mind...

Words Written in the Dark

"We're all human"

Right now
they're trying to pass
a bill
to give people a second chance—
a bipartisan prison reform.
Finally something where both parties are taking a stance.

Haven't you ever made a mistake?
But learned from it and grown?
Time has been served,
and they shouldn't have to be punished for life...
especially if change has been shown.

What a time to be alive.
To witness history that your children's children's children
will soon read in their books... or shall I say iPads.

Use your voice, let it be heard
just as our fighting ancestors had.

ALEXANDRIA RIZIK

"Lost & Found"

I wonder if I'll ever
find it again...
It...
That special thing inside of me,
that I lost.
It was that part of me that loved myself
so deeply.
That part of myself that didn't react
so neurotically.
That part of myself
that didn't assume people were talking about me,
and knew the world was on my side...
Not against me.

I want *it* back.
But you took it...
And didn't even use it.
What a silly thief.

"That's Okay"

We love in different ways—
One way isn't better or worse...
and that's okay.

You see the world in black and grey.
I see it in a colorful array...
and that's okay.

Our funny bones just don't laugh the same,
mine tingles a little more with pain.
And that's okay!

We're just two passengers on the same plane,
temporarily headed in the same direction
but our final destinations are far away...

And that is OKAY.

ALEXANDRIA RIZIK

"Too soon, but I love you"

I want to say it
but I know it's too soon;
I love you
I love you
I love you to the moon.

"Silent Tears"

I cried silent tears
underneath the moon
to the sound of roses,
blooming with new beginnings...

"Dragged to hell"

And now I realize...
I'm the one who got away.
And I would've been dragged to hell
if I had stayed.

"126 Days: the sequel"

126 days since our last goodbye
now you show up in the form of a text message
and you think you deserve a reply?

The crazy part is
I think you do too.
Why does love constantly have a way
of destroying any common sense inside of you?

You're a little too late.
Four months to be exact.
I think I'll make you wait.
I'm stronger now than when you left.

"Erased"

Will we remember yesterday
when the morning light breaks through?
Will we remember last night's "I LOVE YOU"?
What if suddenly our minds are lost and our
brains have erased?
What if we lose every word, every touch, every memory,
that we craved & chased?

Words Written in the Dark

"Second Thoughts..."

I used to think
you hadn't even given me a
second thought...
but now I know
by your random text
and your anger at my delayed reply
that you're more infatuated with me
than I am with you.

And I'm okay with that...

"True Love Always Finds a Way"

A psychic once said
whatever is meant to be
will be
and that it'll never
truly be over
between
you & me.

"Directions"

My mind is pulling me in one direction,
my heart in another.
But my mom said to listen to my gut...
which sits closer to my heart than the other.
What do you do
when your logic and emotions
are running in separate directions?

ALEXANDRIA RIZIK

"Therapy"

"First loves are hard to forget"
at least that's what my therapist says...

"I am not my anxiety"

Is anxiety my identity?
Is that why it's so hard for me
to rid myself of it so quickly?

ALEXANDRIA RIZIK

"Morning Kisses"

Don't try to make me feel special
with your morning kisses
if I'm not the only person
you're kissing...

"I want to be the one"

I want to wish you happy birthday
year after year,
I want to know how your brother is doing
and if he married that girl he once loved so dear.

If we depart,
can we at least stay friends?
Oh, I know,
let's not use that stupid line again...

But seriously,
I want to be the one who you gaze at
walking down the aisle.
I want to be the one who says "I love you too",
not the one who says "it's been a while".

I want to be the one.

ALEXANDRIA RIZIK

"You Can't Explain Chemistry"

They ask what it is
in you that I see.
And I tell them the truth...
you can't explain chemistry.

"I fed you love"

They tease your heart
& fuck with your head
then when you walk away,
they come crawling back,
begging for the love you once fed.

ALEXANDRIA RIZIK

"What if?"

What if Cinderella
didn't forget her shoe?
What do you think
the prince would do?

Could you imagine
if Belle's father
hadn't given her to the beast?
Could anyone else have saved him
during his time of need?

What about Ariel?
What if she hadn't
been tricked into giving up
her voice?
Would fate have given her
another choice?

Sometimes we go through
the bad, to get to the good.
But we can do it!
Even the princesses could.

"Reshaped"

How do we know
who we truly are
if we're continuously changing
and shaping?

ALEXANDRIA RIZIK

"Convenience"

You call
whenever you see
that I'm beginning to forget you…

How convenient.

"Traced"

I want you
to trace your pen
across my page,
& if it hurts,
let me scream with rage.

Blank it begins
until you leave
your mark.
But don't let the story end there...
Please keep writing
& make sure the ink is dark.

You'll forever be embedded into my heart.

ALEXANDRIA RIZIK

"To all the men I once loved"

To all the men
I once loved...
I hope you carry our memories,
I hope they aren't covered in too much blood.

To all the men
who once said my name,
I pray you don't say it now
with anger...in vain.

To all the men
who once made butterflies & other insects
flutter in my stomach,
I know you'll always have a piece of my heart & my respect.

I once loved you. But you weren't the one.

"Catch my heart"

I gave you my heart,
I know it's heavy
but please don't let it fall & break.

If it drops, please catch it.

"Tunnel"

I found the light
and now I'm afraid
to ever live in the dark again...

It's a scary space
walking through a dark tunnel,
unable to see even your two feet in front of you.

"Dark Love"

I know I'll never
feel that
same kind of love
with anyone else...

But I don't know if I want to.

"Surface Level"

Real love
can break down any barrier,
overcome any storm,
and last longer than all the time
that's ever existed and will ever exist.
And if you've never felt that...

You've only ever touched the surface of life.

"First Loves"

First loves…

Embedded in your soul.
Sketched in your mind,
They are a memory never forgotten,
they are a capsule of time.

You can't keep them forever,
as much as you may want.
But you can carry them closely,
inside the depths of your heart.

ALEXANDRIA RIZIK

"Human Nature vs. Human Error"

Love is human nature.
Hate is human error...
and there is a very fine line
between the two.

"Destiny"

I ran away from fate,
because she wouldn't let me have you.
Let's change the path the universe has set,
& be each other's destiny.

ALEXANDRIA RIZIK

"People vs. People"

We personify
love,
cigarettes,
alcohol
as if they kill people...
But it's people that kill one another.
And themselves.

"I am what I am, and I know that I am"

I'm insecure
and it's hard for me to trust,
my heart palpitates when I'm nervous,
and I don't like the feeling of a commitment
or being rushed.

I'm not perfect
and I've had terrible thoughts.
But who the fuck are you
to judge who I am and who I am not?

ALEXANDRIA RIZIK

"The Sun & Midnight"

Some things are just never meant to be;
Like ketchup and ice cream,
the sun and midnight,
You and Me.

Words Written in the Dark

"I don't know how to quit this"

You're my one weakness
and I don't know how to quit this.
Unless you quit me first.

ALEXANDRIA RIZIK

"You were never mine"

For a while, I cried
but then I realized
you were never mine to cry about...

"For a While"

For a while…
my natural hair
was colored
and straightened
and curled
so many times
that it no longer knew
what its natural state was…

        For a while…
        my friends
        were people
        who liked me for
        drinking
        and late nights,
        and the boys I loved
        never treated me right.

                For a while…
                I didn't know
                who I was
                and the choices I made
                decided who I was becoming.
                But now I've left it all behind
                to come back
                to exactly who I've always been
before I colored and straightened and curled my hair.

ALEXANDRIA RIZIK

"Characters"

From every movie I watch
to every book I read,
the characters that fall in love
remind me of you and me.

"Missing"

My heart is in search of repair,
to put all of these pieces back together...
But what will you do
when you see all of the ones that are
missing?

ALEXANDRIA RIZIK

"The Storm"

A storm is coming
and it may be just what I need
to cleanse the wounds
known as *you* and *me*...

"I dreamt of you"

Last night I dreamt of you,
but you weren't you
and I wasn't me,
yet we still found each other in the end,
just like the wind always finds the leaves...

No matter if they are on the ground or on the trees.

ALEXANDRIA RIZIK

"Clouds Made of Flames"

Our love looked like clouds...
but not the kind you see in the sky.
The kind of clouds that result from the flames
of a fire so hot, the whole town walks outside
in the middle of the night
to watch it burn again the midnight sky.
Even if everything crumbles down before them with it...

"Scraped"

What is love?
And why do so many crave it
yet not believe?
Are they scared to fall
and scrape their knees?

I don't need you to catch me...

ALEXANDRIA RIZIK

"Heavenly Answers"

Dear God,

Thank you for having unlimited WiFi.
For always answering your phone
that requires no battery.
And even when you're visiting others,
you answer my call,
never putting it on Airplane Mode.

Thank you for answering
whether it be in the middle of the day,
when you should be busy
or in the middle of the night,
when you could be sleeping.

Thank you, God
for keeping your phone on
and answering all of my prayers.

"Matching Tattoos"

That sound…that song,
it takes me back to that day,
and that smell,
it brings me back to a place
where we once lived
underneath a crescent moon.
Now all that remains
are the matching
tattoos.

ALEXANDRIA RIZIK

"The Places it Hurts"

I want to touch you
in all of the places it hurts
& make you feel again…

"Your Sun is too Strong For Him"

When he says
he isn't looking for light
but then you see him
dancing underneath
another sky's moon,
remember that
it isn't you…
he just wants the one
who lets him continuously
live in the dark.

Your sun is too strong for him.

"Thank You"

The good, the bad…
the moments we can't explain.
If only I had known then,
I'd be grateful, despite the pain.

Lessons and loss,
change and hope…

Today is the day to acknowledge the
experiences and the people
who've helped you grow.

Give thanks & pray.

"Rewritten"

A coffee shop
on a rainy day…
lattes on lips,
words on page.

Our memories seem to be
dancing onto the paper…
into a story
I once lived
and now have to rewrite
the ending.

TBC.

ALEXANDRIA RIZIK

"Anxiety Attack"

Breath caught
in between thoughts,
an appending doom
until all hope is lost…
Accelerated heartbeats
and frantic illusions,
like a mind full of toxic pollution.

"Hoped"

I had hope for you,
but my father always said,
"hope is a bad strategy"…

ALEXANDRIA RIZIK

"Mad like a Storm"

Kiss me
the way the rain
kisses the pavement…
Sometime madly like a storm,
& sometimes gently like a subtle sprinkle,
but always leaving me glowing,
and other reflecting.

"Our Last"

Dance with me
one more dance,
before you dance your first with her
and we have to call this our last…

"A Dozen Roses"

It would take more than
a dozen roses to save this love…
or whatever is left of it.

"My mistake..."

I promised to love you no matter what,
without a promise in return...
my mistake.
Your loss.

ALEXANDRIA RIZIK

"Let somebody else hold the door"

And eventually you just let go,
naturally
like a hand that has been grasping onto a door handle
afraid to close and walk away…
but then you do
and everything is okay.
In fact, it's even better than before
and your hand is no longer strained with something
that brought it pain for much too long.

"26"

(For my mom and dad)

Love at first fight,
it was a special kind of night.
Hospital bound,
he saved her father's life.
Neither of them
would have thought that
they'd found
their husband and wife.

26 years later,
and still going strong
but getting there wasn't easy…
It took a lot of trial and error,
and getting it wrong.

Children
and money,
arguments,
and loss…
No one said it would be a joy ride,
but love can conquer all.

ALEXANDRIA RIZIK

"Gut"

Follow your gut into the wild…

"So fuck yourself"

I was a toy to you,
and you didn't like that I
wasn't broken enough
to put back together….
I was whole
and you, the broken one.
So you took pieces of me
to fill your empty spaces
and made sure I'd never be the same
again.

ALEXANDRIA RIZIK

"Love is patient, but not always kind"

I'll have a soy milk latte,
and a table for two…
although you might not show,
I'll keep waiting for you.

"One in the Same"

Love,
lust...
are they one in the same?
Can you hold the heart of another
without moaning their name?

ALEXANDRIA RIZIK

"Fire Burns Itself"

We started this fire,
we watched it grow.
But like the most beautiful
things in life,
it eventually found its way
back to just logs…

"Thorns"

His lies smelled like roses,
but they made me bleed
like thorns;
I suppose it is
the most beautiful things
that give us life,
yet also hurt us.

ALEXANDRIA RIZIK

"He was a vacation...but you were home"

And I lied next to him
and it felt like a vacation,
but then I lied next to you
and it felt like home…
and I never wanted to leave again.

"Prince Charming"

You will never be my
Prince Charming
or the knight who
slays all my dragons
because I will never
be that girl
who needs someone to slay them...

ALEXANDRIA RIZIK

"Time Flies"

Time flies by
in the blink of an eye…
so wake up early
to catch the sun rise.

"Sticks & Stones"

Whoever said that
sticks and stones may break your bones,
but words cannot hurt you,
must've been a sociopath
because words are more graphic
than the eyes will ever see.
They can be more painful than any
bullet.
Words.
They have more power than a river,
carrying you along with a simple
"I love you"
and dropping you into the depths of the ocean
an anchor tied to your ankle,
with a silent & sudden
"goodbye" —

Words.
They are fuel and poison.

ALEXANDRIA RIZIK

"Poetry is loud"

Writers may be quiet,
but poetry is so very loud…

"Befriending a snake"

You think you want to befriend
a snake,
until you do;
soon you will realize
that in order to be their friend,
you end up with fangs too…

ALEXANDRIA RIZIK

"Love me tender"

Love me tender,
love me fierce,
but promise to never
love me when you no longer do.

"Are we meant to be?"

There's only one of you…
and there's only one of me.
What are the chances
that we are meant to be?

ALEXANDRIA RIZIK

"Kisses and Words"

Kisses.
Words.
Who's to say
they aren't the same thing?
Because I heard more in each
drunken whisper of your tongue
entangled in mine
than anything you were afraid to
ramble in my ear…

"Neurotic Girl's Happily Ever After"

Crackling fire,
the turning page,
these are the sounds
that make my heart beat in beautiful rage.

Kissing lips,
nervous laughter,
the healing sounds
of a neurotic girl's happily ever after.

ALEXANDRIA RIZIK

"The Worst Part"

The worst part about a sad ending…
is knowing how beautiful the beginning was.

"Wasps"

You made me believe those were
butterflies
fluttering around in my stomach
every time we touched…
But they were wasps,
quickly killing me
with every sting.

ALEXANDRIA RIZIK

"Three Organs"

My heart has made me cry
over boys who were never mine.

My mind has been too logical
and said love is simply mythological.

But my gut has never steered me wrong;
it has always warned me of people yet reminded me
that I'm strong.

If only I could get all three of these organs
to get along…

"The Same Bar"

The same bar…
a Saturday night.
Rain painting the street
as the moon strikes it
with its midnight light.

The same bar…
the same person serving drinks,
to the regulars who never left
and never will.

The same bar…
so many memories made,
it feels like home,
but I hope to one day
be the person who walks in
after many years, and everyone
stops to stare and says,
"She's the one who got away".

ALEXANDRIA RIZIK

"Possessed"

You don't own me.

Words Written in the Dark

"Antagonist"

One story's protagonist,
is another story's antagonist.

ALEXANDRIA RIZIK

"Love Isn't Always Romance"

Is love just a component of lust
to validate our ego's desire
to be desired?
Because when we care to look around,
there is already so much love there;
but, apparently, romantic love
is different…

"Human Too"

I think we too often
depend on others,
forgetting that
they're only human too…

"Soulmates"
(for my sisters)

Everyone is in search
of that special person
who they can call their own,
like it's a possession they must keep
so they aren't alone.

I wish they'd stop searching
and see what was right in front of their eyes.
They have so many soulmates,
if they cared to look, they'd be surprised.

I am blessed to say I have three,
they are my sisters,
my best friends,
my secret keepers,
my soulmates…
And our love is forever guaranteed.

"A Happy Poem"

Here's a happy poem,
I hope it makes your day.
Just remember the sun will rise tomorrow
and everything will be okay.

ALEXANDRIA RIZIK

About the Author

Alexandria Rizik is a published writer and award-winning filmmaker, born and raised in Scottsdale, Arizona — where she was brought up by a large Armenian family.

Her love for writing began when she was a young child and her aunt bought her a journal. She told Alexandria to write her a story and the rest is history. Her favorite part about writing is being able to write the *happily ever after* that doesn't always happen in real life.

She received a degree in English from Arizona State University and her published works include her children's book, "Chocolate Milk" and two short stories — "Floral Wallpaper" and "The Writer, the Magician, & the

Psychic", which have been circulated in literary magazines. She also has written articles for many online publications about coping with anxiety, something she pens about from personal experience and plays a large role in her poetry.

Alexandria won best female director at London Independent Film Awards for her short film, "Contentment", in 2017.

Besides writing and film, Alexandria loves yoga, wine, and family time.

Check out Alexandria Rizik on:

www.ingramcontent.com/pod-product-compliance
Lightning Source LLC
LaVergne TN
LVHW041539070426
835507LV00011B/826